The Way
They Should Go

Timeless Advice
for the
Teen Journey

Compiled By
Kirsten Femson
Designed By
Diane RoBlin-Lee

The Way They Should Go: Timeless Advice for the Teen Journey
Copyright ©2006 Kirsten Femson
All rights reserved
Printed in Canada
International Standard Book Number: 1-897186-01-0

Published by:
Castle Quay Books
500 Trillium Drive, Kitchener, Ontario, N2G 4Y4
Tel: (800) 265-6397   Fax (519) 748-9835
E-mail: info@castlequaybooks.com
www.castlequaybooks.com

Copy editing by Diane Roblin-Lee and Marina Hofman
Layout and design by Diane Roblin-Lee
Cover Design by John Cowie, eyetoeye design
Printed at Essence Publishing, Belleville, Ontario

Scripture quotations, unless otherwise indicated, are from the New King James Version of
the Bible, Thomas Nelson Publishers ©1984, 1982, 1980, 1979, and the HOLY BIBLE,
NEW INTERNATIONAL VERSION. Copyright 1973, 1978, 1984 International Bible
Society. Used by permission of Zondervan Bible Publishers.

Library and Archives Canada Cataloguing in Publication

The Way They Should Go: Timeless advice for the teen journey : advice from our nations'
top leaders / [compiled by] Kirsten Femson.

ISBN 1-897186-01-0

        1. Teenagers--Conduct of life. 2. Success in adolescence.
I. Femson, Kirsten, 1989-

BF724.3.S9F42 2006   j158.1'0835   C2005-907573-2

Message from the Publisher

As Kirsten Femson contemplated her Grade Eight Graduation, she dreamt of giving her fellow graduates a special reminder of their years together. What would be the best gift?

Kirsten Femson,
Grade Eight Graduation.

"Wisdom is supreme; therefore, get wisdom. Though it cost all you have, get understanding"
(Proverbs 4:7 NIV).

Armed with over two hundred stamps and envelopes, Kirsten wrote letters to well-known leaders and wise acquaintances, asking them to share words of wisdom and inspiration for her teenage friends.

Then she waited. Before long, stacks of mail began to arrive, bearing the thrilling return addresses of many of her heroes. Over a period of two years, Kirsten and her family happily compiled the responses.

The first edition, a photocopied, cerlox bound masterpiece, was given, with excitement, to each of Kirsten's classmates for graduation.

Never did she dream that her diligence and initiative would go far beyond her classroom to carry words of wisdom to teenagers around the globe.

"Because your love is
Better than life,
my lips will glorify You."

Psalm 63:3 (NIV)

4

Foreword

As you begin to read this book, it is my prayer that the words and thoughts contained within will be meaningful to you. This book represents the beliefs and convictions of people from divergent walks of life and diverse age groups. Each contributor has composed thoughts from his or her heart and I trust that these words will challenge your heart and your mind.

Some messages were written to my Grade Eight Class when they graduated in June 2003. Others were written more recently. Each of these messages were collected over a three year period as I put this book together so that the wise advice could be shared more widely.

Although contributors did not know the content or writing of others, there are some resounding themes throughout what has been written. Contributors challenge you as a reader to:

* Believe in yourself and who God made you;
* Be respectful of the beliefs of others;
* Do your best to grow academically and spiritually every day;
* Strive for excellence;
* Step out and take risks;
* Have a conscience for your community;
* Count friends as a valuable resource;
* Set daily goals that will guide your work; and
* Never give up on your dreams.

As you read the following contributions, may you be built up and encouraged, challenged and enlightened.

Kirsten Femson

Acknowledgements

The compilation of this book has been a wonderful learning journey for my family and myself. I would like to thank Mr. Ogborne, Principal of the Pickering Christian School, who was encouraging from the first moment. Little did we know what God would have in store ~ that the work would continue and be published.

My heartfelt appreciation goes to all of the contributors. Each time a new submission arrived, I was so excited. My family and I would read them over together and enjoy each word. My gratitude goes to each one for the words of wisdom and for investing the time in sharing insights to encourage others. May these words encourage each person who reads what has been written.

Thanks to my family who helped me organize letters, prepare and address envelopes, type submissions and keep all the files in order. Even my little sister helped by putting stamps on outgoing and return envelopes and running to retrieve whatever we needed.

Much appreciation goes to Mr. Larry Willard, my publisher, who took me on as a potential writer, when I was only 14. Each time we met with Mr. Willard, I went home with new knowledge and feeling valued. He made me feel at ease and instilled in me confidence that the goal would be accomplished. Thank you Mr. Willard for liberally sharing your knowledge, and for your caring perspective, guidance and encouraging emails. You made this all possible.

We have prayed from the beginning of this project that each contributor and reader would be greatly blessed as they read the entries. This means that if you happen to be reading this book, we have been praying for you.

Blessings to each of you,
Kirsten Femson

"A word aptly spoken
is like apples of gold
in settings of silver."

Proverbs 25:11 (NIV)

Contributors

To every man there openeth
A way, and ways, and a way.
And the high soul climbs the high way,
And the low soul gropes the low:
And in between, on the misty flats,
The rest drift to and fro.
But to every man there openeth
A high way and a low,
And every man decideth.
The way his soul shall go.

John Oxenham

Philip Arkoh-Forson

Vice Principal Dunbarton High School, Pickering, Ontario

My parents were divorced when I was three and I was brought up by my maternal grandma in West Africa. She passed her faith in God and His Son Jesus Christ on to me and I have loved Him from childhood.

Without a father figure to look up to, I had a vacuum inside that motivated me to find a mentor. I looked up to my teachers, choir directors and pastors. I served anyone who was willing to coach me about life. **I learned that you cannot serve God without serving the people He brings your way.** These men taught me to pray; to serve without grumbling; to take rebuke with humility; and to study.

Do you want promotion in life? The fear of the Lord is the starting point. Pray. Humble yourself to leadership and authority. Serve without grumbling. Take rebuke and correction. Have hope. Work hard at every good thing your hands find to do. Study as if there is no tomorrow.

Note to Self

You will face challenges in life, but with the solid foundation that you will build by doing these things, you will stand the storms. You are in for a ball!

Kay Arthur
Author, Teacher

"I think it would be so good if every morning, before we ever put our feet on the floor or rise from our bed, we would make the conscious decision that this day, no matter what the discipline, the cost, we are going to live for Christ. It would be the first commitment of the day, spoken aloud ~ a confession with our mouths from our hearts".

Source: Arthur, K. (2001). Lord, Give Me A Heart For You: A Devotional Study on Having a Passion for God. Colorado: WaterBrook Press, p. 113. Used by permission

Darrell Baker

Pastor of Faith Baptist Church, Huntsville, Ontario

It is becoming increasingly important that we know what we believe. The traditional view of family, of marriage, of even right and wrong is no longer a "given" in our world today. More and more people are questioning beliefs and standards that have been the foundation of civilization for thousands of years.

The only source of truth that we possess that has not, and will not change, is the Bible. Jesus said, "*I tell you the truth, until heaven and earth disappear, not the smallest letter, not the least stroke of a pen, will by any means disappear from the Law until everything is accomplished*" (Matthew 5:18, NIV).

Know what you believe, know the Bible, and know Jesus personally.

18

Norma Barker
Grandmother

You may not think that choices you make have any great consequences ~ not flossing properly, playing certain sports to such intensity that injury results, not eating properly, making wrong moral choices.

Take a hard look at the adults you know. Observe the need for a root canal, chiropractic visits, and expensive treatments. Observe the regrets and hurts that often last a lifetime.

Make the tough choices now. Learn to practise a healthy lifestyle. Establish good routines. Learn to be honest and give God first place in your life. Prepare to enjoy your life more fully as an adult!

Note to Self

Ken Blewett
Property Manager,
Pickering Christian School

Your life will undergo many changes. Because of human frailties and weaknesses you sometimes might feel apprehensive and uncertain when change knocks at your door. You may even feel like trembling as you think of your future.

You may feel like trembling because you are starting to venture out from the comfortable stage of your life where your parents surrounded you with love, and gave you guidance and protection. You are starting a new and unknown stage, filled with challenges and uncertainties. And you may feel like trembling because you will be starting to think of your future ~ your goals and your career and where you want to be in the next five, ten and 20 years.

But you are maturing and you are becoming wiser. You will begin to understand your strengths and your capabilities. You might then think of Stephen Hopkins, when he was faced with signing the Declaration of Independence and said, "...but my heart does not tremble."

Your heart will not tremble because you have the resources of your parents, your family, your friends and/or your teachers to draw upon to help you continue your education and help you make the important decisions that will face you in the future.

20

And your heart will not tremble because wherever life takes you and whatever decisions you make, you can be content with the knowledge that your Saviour Jesus Christ is at your side to encourage you and to protect you. The Bible says in Job 8:7 that if you trust in the Lord, "Your beginnings will seem humble, so prosperous will your future be."

As with Hopkins, if you fill your heart with courage and resolve, your future will be bright and wonderful.

Laurence Sterne once said "What a large volume of adventures may be grasped within this little span of life by him who interests his heart in everything." **Let your interests be broad. Let every moment be a learning experience. Let your heart be content. Trust in God.**

References:

1) "My hand trembles, but my heart does not." McCullough, David. John Adams. New York: Touchstone, Simon & Schuster 2002 p.138

2) "Your beginnings will seem humble, so prosperous will your future be" Job 8:7, The NIV Study Bible. New International Version. Grand Rapids: Zondervan Bible Publishers. 1985

3) "What a large volume of adventures may be grasped within this little span of life by him who interests his heart in everything." McCullough, David. John Adams. New York: Touchstone, Simon & Schuster, 2002 p.287

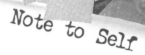

Note to Self

21

Note to Self

22

Marg Blewett
Teacher, Pickering Christian School

Proverbs 3: 5&6 says, "Trust in the Lord with all your heart and lean not on your own understanding; in all your ways acknowledge Him, and He will make your paths straight."

Imagine all these years accumulating skills, knowledge and wisdom ~ only to be reminded that you have a finite mind that must continually depend on a Creator, a Creator that passionately loves you and wants to be part of your every day. He wants to bless you with straight paths that He walks with you, hand in hand.

Be wise, develop a personal, passionate relationship with your God.

23

Dr. Kenneth D. Boa

President, Reflections Ministries and Trinity House Publishers, Atlanta, Georgia

Here is a list of forty personal principles and values that I have collected and review from time to time. It is convicting for me to go through these, since they are all beyond my experience. This list may be of use to you as you seek to integrate your life in Christ with your life in the world.

1 Faith: a radical trust in the sovereignty and goodness of God. God is in control and has my best interests at heart.

2 Hope: anchored in the promises of God.

3 Love: a deepening love for God (mind, emotions, will, actions) based on growing intimacy with Him.

4 The temporal versus the eternal ~ **I must treat the temporal as temporal and the eternal as eternal by esteeming the invisible over the visible.**

5 More than anything else, a passion to know God.

6 Compassion for the lost.

7 Since I cannot live on yesterday's faith, I must be willing to take greater risks based on God's character and promises.

8 A growing awareness of my profound need for grace in all things.

9 A clearer understanding of the truth that my deepest needs are met in Christ, so that I am secure enough to serve others without manipulating relationships to get my needs met.

10 Developing a spirit of humility, complete dependence, and teachability.

11 A willingness to forgive others as Christ has forgiven me.

12 Treating people with grace, dignity, and possibility.

13 A stewardship mentality ~ increased awareness of God's ownership of all things and an attitude of contentment in all things.

14 Commitment to ongoing exercise and renewal of spirit, soul, and body.

15 Personal integrity ~ a congruence between the inside and the outside.

16 Openness and honesty in relationships.

This is a pretty long list, Doc!

Herb

Note to Self

17 Radical commitment to the Great Commandment.

18 Radical commitment to the Great Commission.

19 Standing firm in the spiritual warfare by submitting to God and resisting the lures of the world, the flesh, and the devil.

20 Practicing Christ's presence in all things and doing everything to His glory.

21 Accountability to godly people and a willingness to respond with humility to exhortation and rebuke so that I will not be enmeshed in self-deception.

22 Maintaining a sense of childlike wonder and awe.

23 Focusing on the process and not the product; genuine ministry flows out of who I am in Christ.

24 Walking in the power of the Spirit and putting no confidence in the flesh.

25 Being fully alive to the present and not living in the past or the future.

26 Living each day as though it were my last, and treating

Note to Self

relationships in the same way. Cultivating the mentality of a sojourner, pilgrim, stranger, and alien as I wait expectantly for my true home.

27 Growing responsiveness and sensitivity to God's loving initiatives.

28 An ongoing attitude of thanksgiving and joy that transcends my circumstances. A willingness to cling to God's character in the midst of life's pains and pleasures.

29 Manifesting the fruit of the Spirit by abiding in Christ.

30 A commitment to ongoing renewal of the mind so that I can grow in intimacy with God and not be seduced by the culture.

31 An increased willingness to live out the truth that everything God asks me to do is for my ultimate good, and that everything He asks me to avoid is detrimental to my soul.

32 An awareness that good and evil both increase at compound interest, and a corresponding desire to live in the light of Luke 16:10.

33 A desire to give my life in exchange for the things God declares to be important; a willingness to define success by the standard of the Word (relational) and not by the standard of the world (functional).

34 The pursuit of godly mentors who are farther along in the spiritual journey.

35 An understanding that habits of holiness are sustained by discipline and dependence; unholy habits are sustained by default.

36 I must be faithful to the process and let go of ownership of the results.

37 A firm belief that since the ministry cannot be measured, I must be content with what God has given me and not compare my ministry with others.

38 Asking God for the three faithful wounds of contrition, compassion, and longing after God.

39 Continued and responsible cultivation of giftedness while at the same time depending less on knowledge and skills and more on the power of the Holy Spirit.

40 Commitment to the centrality of Christ in all I am and do.

Harry Bollback

Co-founder of Word of Life.

If you can learn the 3 A's, it will enrich your life, help you in the time of decision to accept whatever God brings into your life..

Psalm 37:3 Trust in the Lord. ACCEPT whatever He brings into your life. You can trust Him.

Psalm 37:4 Delight yourself in the Lord. Get a good ATTITUDE about what He brings into your life. You can't change it, so get a "God" attitude about it.

Wise, eh? (Get it???)

Psalm 37:5 Commit your way to the Lord. Make all the necessary ADJUSTMENTS. He hasn't failed anybody yet and you are not important enough for God to make history over you.

Word of life fellowship, inc.

Note to Self

Rev. Joe Boot
Christian Apologist,
Author and Educator

Kirsten Femson and Joe Boot

Having an education and a head full of knowledge does not mean we have wisdom. Information and wisdom are different things altogether. Many of the most intelligent people in history have also been utterly foolish and some have been tyrants.

True knowledge comes from the Lord. So to honor God is the very first rung on the ladder of wisdom. This means that we must fill our minds with sound knowledge to grow in understanding. This is found, first and foremost, in God's Word. The foundation of God's Word in Christ as revealed in all of Scripture comes to us with God's authority. Christ tells us that the wise build upon this rock.

If you want to be a person of understanding and wisdom who can handle all that life will throw at you and if you want to know the pleasantness of true knowledge, I can think of no more important council than that which I received as a child that has kept me safe in life and guided my path:
"The fear of the Lord is the beginning of wisdom."
(Proverbs 9:10).

Note to Self

31

Rev. Cal R. Bombay
Author, Missionary, Television Broadcaster

"Wisdom is the principal thing; therefore get wisdom. And in all your getting, get understanding" (Proverbs 4:7).

We live in an age when true wisdom is lacking. Yet it is the principal thing. It should be our greatest quest. It must be at the top of our 'wish' list, yet it cannot be had by wishing. It can only be had by a diligent seeking after God. Above everything else, including riches and fame, Solomon asked God for wisdom. We read in Ecclesiastes 7:25 the value of practical wisdom: *"I applied my heart to know, to search and seek out wisdom and the reason of things, to know the wickedness of folly, even of foolishness and madness."*

Never be afraid to ask questions. Everything about our life, our world and our universe is both created by God and understood through the wisdom that God gives. Sometimes we understand things by faith, and that too is great wisdom.

For any true understanding of the world around us, we must be in a right relationship with God. Theories, ideas and propositions, which sound good, may even come from the greatest of intellects, but until they are purified through the cauldron of God's

32

Word, and the wisdom of His Word, none of them will stand the test of time. In Proverbs 11:30 we read: "The fruit of the righteous is a tree of life, and he who wins souls is wise."

Life will throw some severe curves at you, but every one of them can be handled if we trust the source, and use the wisdom that God freely gives. "If any of you lacks wisdom, let him ask of God, who gives to all liberally and without reproach, and it will be given to him" (James 1:5).

Note to Self

33

Dr. Bill Bright

Founder and Chairman,
Campus Crusade for Christ International.

Dr. Bright

I want to commend you for your commitment to our wonderful Lord and Savior, Jesus Christ. Your decision to love, trust and obey Him is the most important decision you will ever make after the assurance of your salvation. Your studies about how to live for and please God will be of invaluable aid as you learn to serve Him.

Let me encourage you with this thought ~ you are never too young to commit yourselves completely to Christ. **God has often used people as young as you are to accomplish amazing things for His kingdom.** He wants to use you in ways you could never imagine. He just asks that you believe in Him, and commit yourselves to His ways.

Please always remember the words our Lord Jesus gave to His followers: "... No one has ever given up anything: home, brothers, sisters, mother, father, children, or property for love of Me and to tell others the Good News, who won't be given back, a hundred times over....!" (Mark 10:29-30 TLB).

My hope is that you will experience our wonderful Lord and trust Him in greater and greater ways. May He bless you and all you endeavor on His behalf!

34

Photos on this page of Dr Bright and his students cou of Campus Crusade for Ch International..

Dr. D. Stuart Briscoe
Minister-at-Large, Elmbrook Church

"A friend of mine is an eminent research physician. One day she told me, "In my field, our technology is out stepping our ethic." She was addressing a problem we all face! **Because I could does not mean I should.** And then because I should does not mean I would! She said, "I need wisdom from above to sort it all out!!" So do we all."

Note to Self

35

Sandra Brown
Friend of Kirsten

Obtain the best education you possibly can and pursue and attain your goals in life. Listen to your parents and older relatives or friends (they know more than you think they do) and consider their advice carefully.

The pathway through life won't always be smooth. We were never promised that. But if you will remember to **keep your eyes upon Jesus**, and no matter what obstacles and difficulties may come your way ~ no matter what the pressures ~ He will guide you through.

Steve Brown
Bible Teacher on Key Life

Remember two things:

First God really does really love you far beyond your imagination ~ and nothing can ever change that. In fact, **there is absolutely nothing you can do to get God to love you one iota more than He already does and there is absolutely nothing you can do to get God to love you one iota less.** "Who shall separate us from the love of Christ?...For I am convinced that neither death nor life ...neither the present or the future ... neither height nor depth, nor anything else in all creation, will be able to separate us from the love of God that is in Christ Jesus our Lord" (Romans 8:35-39).

Second, **God really does have a perfect plan and purpose just for you ~ right now and in the future.** "'For I know I have the plans I have for you,' declares the Lord, 'plans to prosper you and not to harm you, plans to give you a hope and the future'" (Jeremiah 29:11). You're in God's hands...and He can always be trusted.

Note to Self

Rev. Ian Campbell

Senior Pastor, Bramalea Baptist Church

Although you think of your lives as spreading out ahead of you in long spans of years and decades, the truth is that the commitments you make now will shape all of those years and decades.

Two things are very important commitments that will shape your lives.

One ~ **your character, which is years in the making, can be lost in a moment.** Always hold on to the moral and ethical commitments you have made as a young follower of Jesus. Those will be your greatest asset and provide your greatest impact on your generation and world. In this matter be leaders, not followers.

Two ~ in this matter be followers, not leaders ~ God's glory and His kingdom are of the utmost importance. Life is not about me, it is about God. What does He want? What does He want me to do? I must follow Him, not expect Him to follow me.

Note to Self

38

Dr. Tony Campolo
Professor Emeritus of Sociology, Author, Speaker

Tony Campolo

Don't be afraid to attempt something great and remember there is nothing of significance that doesn't require a great deal of risk-taking. Set your sights high ~ because that is what the stars are for.

As you get your education, remember that education is not so much a privilege as it is a responsibility. Most people in the world will not have the education that you have at your disposal. Study to show yourself approved unto God. Use your education to benefit others. Remember that the purpose of going to school is not to get the credentials, to secure the position that will enable you to earn a great deal of money so that you can buy a lot of "stuff" that you really don't need. The purpose of an education is to equip you to better live out a commitment of service to God and to God's people in the world. The Bible says that to whom much is given, from them much is expected. You have been given much and much is expected from you.

These are crucial times, and who can say otherwise but that **God created you and placed you at this particular time and place because there is something special that you are ordained to do.** Don't miss out on that greatness.

Note to Self

40

Rev. Jim Cantelon
Author/Broadcaster

In Africa, where my wife and I work with HIV/AIDS orphans and widows, we meet a lot of real heroes. Usually they're women. Without income they often care for as many as twenty orphans. They work all day at some menial task to barter their labors for

Jim & Kathy Cantelon

food and they care for the children. They look twice their age. And they live without help or hope.

Yet they keep at it. They don't give up. Every day they show up for work. Every day they mother the orphans. And they do a terrific job.

They have taught me something very important: **worthwhile loving requires that we "show up" and "keep at it". Wherever you are, BE THERE.**

W. D. T. Carter
Lawyer

Never give up on your dreams, your family, your faith or yourself.

Golden Rule
Luke 6:31

Do to others
as you would
have them do
to you.

The Hon. Elinor Caplan
Former Minister of National Revenue, Ottawa, Canada

Elinor Caplan

CSI
Canada Strategies Inc.

Each endeavor, whether exciting or painful, should be pursued with the goal of achieving excellence. If you are proud of your effort, you will succeed.

When you make a decision, "GO FOR IT". If you find it isn't right for you, make a change. Life is too short to live afraid. Embrace life's opportunities to the fullest.

There are no short-cuts to success. Work hard. Be a good and loyal friend. Be ready to learn from everyone. Never be afraid to question. Always be prepared for criticism. If you stumble, pick yourself up, dust yourself off and hold your head high.

The Golden Rule is found in the scriptures of nearly every religion and is rightly considered the code of human conduct and ethics. "Treat others as you would have them treat you and yours."

Be clear about what you value and your values. I have never cried over anything that cannot shed a tear. Things can be replaced. Lives cannot be replaced.

Never be afraid to ask for forgiveness instead of waiting for permission to do that which is good. When you err or hurt others, apologize.

Count your blessings often. Above all, never take your democracy, your rights or your freedom for granted.

Note to Self

43

Claire Carver Dias
Olympic Bronze Medallist (Synchronized Swimming)

Claire Carver Dias

God wants all of us to live up to our greatest potential. When we were created, God instilled talents, dreams and special abilities in all of us. Our job is to do all we can to develop

those talents and pursue those dreams. One of the best ways we can reach our potential is to learn how to set and pursue goals. When I was training for the 2000 Olympic Games, my coach taught me the value of setting and pursuing small daily goals that would help me work my way towards achieving my large dream goal of having a medal performance at the Games.

I kept an in-depth daily goal book where I chronicled my goals, struggles and triumphs. The goal book helped me sort out my thoughts and feelings and develop effective strategies to reach my goals.

I encourage all of you to **grab a hold of your dreams by taking the time to set goals for your life. Start a daily goal book of your own.** Take your

goals seriously. Surround yourself with positive people who will encourage you to be your best. Talk honestly to God about your dreams and goals ~ He will be your greatest cheerleader.

44

Michael Coren
Author and Broadcaster

Kirsten with Michael Coren

As we go through life we must remember that **we are not mere individuals, but creatures, made by God who loves us and as such, expects certain things from us such as love, responsibility, wisdom, effort and devotion to Him and His Son Yeshua.** We have to live with the knowledge that we are broken people and that we will sometimes fail in our efforts, but that we must never give up working for the common good, seeking justice and trying to bring people closer to the truth and knowledge of Christ. Every person we meet is vulnerable, even if they hurt us. Forgive, love and remain firm and strong. This is only the land of shadows, real life has not begun yet.

Note to Self

Chuck Colson

Founder, Prison Fellowship Ministries
Message to the Graduating Class 2003
Pickering Christian School

PRISON
FELLOWSHIP.
Ministries

As you may know, I achieved success at an early age ~ at least by the world's standards. I earned a scholarship through Brown University and graduated with honors. Then, I earned a Juris Doctor degree at night, again with honors. I served as a company commander in the Marines; was the youngest administrative assistant in the United States Senate; became a senior partner in a large and thriving law firm; and at the age 39, was named an assistant to the President, sitting in the office immediately next to his. I was the grandson of an immigrant and my life was the American dream fulfilled.

It was only when I achieved all of those things that I realized how empty they really were. I was seeking to find meaning in life through power, influence, money, stature and politics, and I failed. I had success, but I also had a tremendous hole inside of me. I discovered that it was a spiritual vacuum. Later, in prison with all the things of this world stripped away, I found the only security and meaning and purpose a person ever knows ~ a personal relationship with the living God, Jesus Christ.

Looking back, I can honestly say that I never met anyone the entire time I was in government who told me that their

life had been affected by anything I had done ~ at least for the good. By contrast, I've met hundreds, maybe thousands, since I've been in Christian service, whose lives God has chosen to touch through my life and virtually through my biggest defeat, going to prison

Today, how would I define success? Certainly not the way I did in the first forty years of my life. Now, **success to me is believing, following and serving God, and being at peace with Him**. I keep a plaque on my desk that reminds me of what I believe to be the principal calling of the Christian. It reads:

"Faithfulness Not Success."

Reprinted with permission of Prison Fellowship, www.pfm.org

47

Don Cousens
Mayor, Town of Markham

You and I are very privileged to be Canadians. We have not experienced the conditions and poverty of Third World young people and families. Many people survive on less than $1.00 a day.

Overall, one third of the world's population is under the age of 15, and 85 percent of these children live in Third World countries. We can hardly imagine the conditions others live in. Many live on the streets or fight as underage soldiers, or are exploited for their labor or bodies. More than 30,500 children under the age of 5 are dying daily from diseases that can be prevented.

I am proud to support and be a member of the Board of Directors of World Vision, an international humanitarian aid organization that works with the poor and oppressed. World Vision, along with many other organizations, helps people realize a better future.

As you look beyond your own comfortable home and neighborhood, **take the time to remember and support those who are less fortunate** ~ through organizations serving people's needs across the globe. This shows compassion and leadership, two important qualities that give more meaning to your life.

48

Evelyn Cowan
Friend of kirsten

You are entering into a wider world with bigger activities where you will need to make wise decisions. There will be peer pressure. It is well to listen and not argue, but don't be persuaded against your better judgment.

There will be interruptions along the way in your routine, plans and dreams. It may be because of health, money or family situations. These perceived interruptions can open the door to unexpected opportunities, depending on how you deal with the challenges. They can be learning processes to refine, shape and perfect you, regardless of disappointment and tears. Sometimes your reaction will be to get even, but you must forgive and not harbor hate. Reach out and encourage others. **Life is like a race ~ we get tired and want to quit but we must keep on going on**

Note to Self

49

Nicky Cruz

Speaker, Author

I want to share something very important that I have learned ~ the most powerful words that can make the biggest difference in our lives...love and forgiveness. These two walk hand in hand.

Love, I discovered on the streets of New York City. No one on this earth can kill love. God is love ~ unconditional love ~ no matter what! There is no changing God's love ~ accept it.

The journey to healing is through forgiveness. I learned in my youth the only way to break through the dark cloud of pain is to forgive. Forgiveness is not a feeling, it's a choice. Your heart can betray you, causing you to feel "up" one day and "down" the next. It is possible that you can feel depressed because of the way your heart can change. It is important for your spiritual sanity to exercise your choice and to forgive. Forgiveness also means you give up the right to hurt others when you have been hurt.

Nicky Cruz.

Love is a healing force. That and the power to forgive are ours thanks to God through Jesus Christ our Savior.

Lorna Dueck

Journalist, Author, Broadcaster, Listen Up TV

God wants you to enjoy Him and His beautiful world. Everything good was created for God's glory and that means you. Next to God, people are the most precious treasure you will ever encounter. Stay glued to your Bibles, to learn that wise people are peace makers, gentle, kind and honest. (James 3)

It will puzzle you that life will require you to be stubborn and persistent, fighting hard to remain kind and gentle, yet not giving up on trying hard to live as a Christian. Pray for a godly mentor in your life at all times. **Be a listener, a learner, a student of life that carries Joshua 1:8-9 with you at all times.**

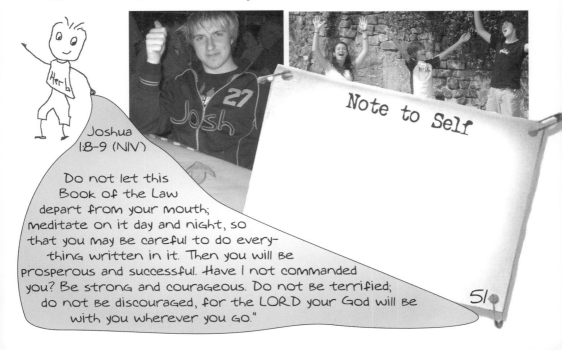

Joshua 1:8-9 (NIV)

Do not let this Book of the Law depart from your mouth; meditate on it day and night, so that you may be careful to do everything written in it. Then you will be prosperous and successful. Have I not commanded you? Be strong and courageous. Do not be terrified; do not be discouraged, for the LORD your God will be with you wherever you go."

Note to Self

Dr. James Dobson
Founder, Focus on the Family

"As Solomon grew old, his wives turned his heart after other gods, and his heart was not fully devoted to the Lord his God, as the heart of David his father had been. He followed Ashtoreth the goddess of the Sidonians, and Molech the detestable god of the Ammonites. So Solomon did evil in the eyes of the Lord; he did not follow the Lord completely, as David his father had done" (I Kings 11:4-6).

Now we know why Solomon was so depressed in the latter years of his life. He had a dark stain on his heart that was like a cancer gnawing at his insides. He had betrayed the God of his father, David. Can't you see the king bowing face down before the false gods of Ashtoreth and Molech? These idols were used by pagan nations for the most unthinkable wickedness, including orgies and the sacrifice of innocent children. Yet Solomon, who had conversed with God and received every good gift from His hand, persisted in worshiping these evil symbols. Then he enticed the people of Israel to do likewise. Consequently, Solomon had lost all meaning in life, which explains his boredom with riches, fame, women, slaves, accomplishments, gold, and even laughter. God's hand was no longer on him.

The lesson for the rest of us is clear. If we ignore the Lord and violate His commandments, there will be no meaning for us, either. The temporal things

of this world, even vast riches and power, will not deliver the satisfaction they advertise!

There must be something more substantial on which to base one's values, purposes, and goals. And of course there is. Jesus said it succinctly:

"But seek ye **first** the kingdom of God, and His righteousness: and all these things shall be added unto you" (Matthew 6:33 KJV).

I rest my case.

Excerpt from:
Life on the Edge: A Young Adult's Guide to a Meaningful Future © 1995, James Dobson, Inc. P.67-68.

Used by permission of Multnomah Publishers Inc.

Note to Self

54

The Hon. Janet Ecker

Former Ontario Minister of Finance, Minister of Education

You will have many new beginnings in your life. Treat each one of them as an opportunity to start afresh. Ask yourself what did I learn about life in the previous chapter and how will that experience help me do better in the next one.

No matter what your dreams or goals, you can achieve them with hard work, strong faith and determination. Most importantly, take advantage of every opportunity to learn about yourself and the world around you, because in the end, your mind is the best gift that God has given you.

Note to Self

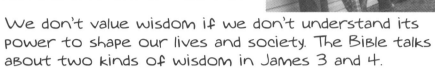

Albert Ehmann
International Director of World Team

We don't value wisdom if we don't understand its power to shape our lives and society. The Bible talks about two kinds of wisdom in James 3 and 4.

One kind of wisdom produces fights, quarrels, chaos and destruction. It comes from envy and selfish ambition. The Bible calls it devilish.

In contrast, the wisdom that comes from God is pure, peace-loving, considerate, submissive, full of mercy, and produces a harvest of goodness.

Think carefully about the kind of wisdom you will choose. If at home, school or work you find yourself in the midst of chaos and quarrels, remember that you don't have to live that way. You can choose to live by a higher and better wisdom that God offers you.

Note to Self

Pastor David Epstein
Senior Pastor, Calvary Baptist Church, New York City

True wisdom is the power of understanding. **Wisdom produces freedom; not the freedom to do anything I want, but the power to do everything God wants.** I find the greatest example of this wisdom and power and freedom in Jesus, the wisest person who ever lived. In Colossians 2:3, it says, *"In Christ are hidden all the treasures of wisdom and knowledge."* Therefore, the greatest wisdom and power and freedom comes from God through a friendship with Jesus.

Power! yeah, man!

Herb

57

Robert Elmer
Author

My Grade Eight English teacher, Mr. Little, taught me about the power of the written word. He taught me that when you write something down it keeps going and going. And he wrote something in my yearbook I would never forget: "I expect to read or teach something of yours, someday." Now I can pass along the same challenge to you today, even if we've never met.

The challenge? **Tell your story, no matter how crazy things are out there, and no matter what you hear on the news.** No matter how much evil there is, or how much war, Christians have a story to tell.

So tell your story, whether you end up selling tents or fixing teeth. In writing? Great. Over the phone? Terrific In a song? Beautiful. Over the backyard fence? Whatever works. Tell about how God has worked in your life. Who else is going to sell it for you? Just don't be silent. Don't be quiet. The world needs to know.

I pray that each of us will learn to tell that precious story in new, creative ways. So, sharpen your pencils, and God's best to you!

Susan Elmer

Kirsten's Teacher, French and English, 2003

Students at our school often write scripture verses on their binders, assignments and tests. There was a Grade 7 French student who would always write Philippians 4:13 on her tests before she would begin. It is so wonderful to see the spiritual progress she has made from hoping that God would help her to succeed, to knowing that He would be faithful to her as she put her heart and soul into every assignment she was given. She has learned to internalize God's truth and fully trust Him to supply her every need.

As a teacher, I have learned some very valuable lessons from my students. I have learned that failure can sometimes be a good thing. It's fear of failure that can be so paralyzing because it keeps us from taking risks and growing in our faith. Striving to be the best we can be through our relationship with Jesus Christ guarantees true contentment.

Note to Self

Leila Femson
Kirsten's Nana

The Oxford dictionary defines wisdom as "experience and knowledge together with sagacious judgement." Sagacious is defined as "having or showing insight or good judgement." Davis' Dictionary of the Bible states that wisdom is "one of the three departments of knowledge among the Hebrews." Wisdom seeks by observation, experience and reflection to know things in their essence and reality as they stand related to man and God".

You stand at a major crossroad of your life where many of you will have to decide whether to live God's way or your own way. The world's way is very, very tempting and the road is very wide. God's way is a narrow road. A Christian's home is in heaven. We are just occupying or passing through this world.

To obtain wisdom you have to know the will of God for your life. To know it:
1. Read your Bible daily
2. Meditate or think on God's word
3. Pray daily
4. Seek wise counsel from Godly people.

Note to Self

The Pocket Oxford Dictionary. New Edition. 1978. Sixth Edition. Oxford at The Clarendon Press. P. 1041.

A Dictionary of the Bible by John D. Davis. 4th Rev. Edition Baker Book House, Grand Rapids 6, Michigan 1958. p. 821

kirsten and Lauren

Lauren Femson
Kirsten's (seven-year-old) Sister

You should pay attention in school and do your homework. You should never be selfish. You must always tell the truth and be nice to your friends. It is important that you obey your mom and dad because God commands this. In Exodus 20:12 it tells us, "Honor your mother and your father, so that you may live long in the land the Lord your God is giving you." (NIV) In Junior Kindergarten I learned that Jonah didn't obey the Lord and he wasted a lot of time before he listened to God. So, when God tells you to do something, just do it.

Michael R. Femson
Kirsten's Father, Realtor

My parents prayed daily for me that God would give me wisdom, understanding and discernment. My mother now prays for wisdom for our daughters in all aspects of their lives. As you consider decisions throughout your life, pray for God's direction and leading.

Spurgeon said and I quote, "Wisdom is the right use of knowledge. To know is not to be wise. Many men know a great deal, and are all the greater fools for it. There is no fool so great a fool as a knowing fool. But to know how to use knowledge is to have wisdom."

Ask God to liberally give you wisdom so that you can stick handle through life's daily obstacles. James 3, verses 13-17 (NIV) says that there are two kinds of wisdom: "Who is wise and understanding among you? Let him show it by his good life, by deeds done in the humility that comes from wisdom. But if you harbor bitter envy and selfish ambition in your hearts, do not boast about it or deny the truth. Such "wisdom" does not come down from heaven but is earthly, unspiritual, of the devil. For where you have envy and selfish ambition, there you find

Note to Self

disorder and every evil practice. But the wisdom that comes from Heaven is first of all pure; then peace-loving, considerate, submissive, full of mercy and good fruit, impartial and sincere".

Develop daily habits that include reading God's word because that is how He speaks to you. Pray daily because this is how you speak to Him and thank Him for all your blessings.

With all your heart seek enthusiastically, passionately and uncompromisingly after God's wisdom for every aspect of your life.

The Forbes Leadership Library: Thoughts on Wisdom: Thoughts and Reflections from History's Great Thinkers. Triumph Books: Chicago, p.57.

Dr. Michael Green
Author and Broadcaster

"The fear of the Lord is the beginning of wisdom." Those words sound old-fashioned. They are not cool. But they are true. The longer I live the clearer I am that **there is no foundation for life which compares with putting God in the center.**

Note to Self

65

Elisabeth Elliot Gren
Author, Broadcaster, www.elisabethelliot.org

If there's one subject that young people ask me about more than any other, it's "How can I know what God wants me to do?"

How do we get guidance from God?

Psalm 143:8b-10 says, "Show me the way I should go, for to you I lift up my soul. Rescue me from my enemies, O Lord, for I hide myself in you. Teach me to do your will, for you are my God; may your good Spirit lead me on level ground."

There are three primary requirements in receiving the guidance of God:

#1. **Trust**. You have got to trust in the Shepherd. Do you really believe that the God of the universe is trustworthy ~ for the tiniest details of your life?
#2 **Obey**. The old hymn says, "There's no other way to be happy in Jesus, but to trust and obey."
#3. **Do faithfully what God wants you to do today.**

In short: tell God you'll do what He says. Read your Bible and pray. (How are you going to know what He's saying if you don't read your Bible and pray?) Do the next thing ~ whatever your duties are.

Ruth F. Harper
Kirsten's Nana

Cherish and nurture the friendships you have made throughout the years at school; they may prove to be lifelong treasures.

Several years ago, I reconnected with an old school friend I hadn't heard from in many years. We played together as children beginning at age three and attended the same schools, usually in the same class. Since reconnecting, I hear from my friend at Christmas with a warm greeting as well as on our birthdays when we send cards or speak by telephone. Our common past provides much material for pleasurable reminiscing.

I thank God for other special friendships that have enriched my life in the dark lonely days that followed the death of my beloved husband of 47 years. Thank God for friends!

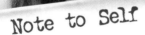

Note to Self

67

Frances Harper
Auntie Fran — Kirsten's Great Aunt

At almost 80 years of age, I look back upon life which has had its joys as well as sorrows, and can say from my heart, "What a wonderful Saviour is Jesus, my Lord. I will be forever grateful to the friend who invited me to church when we were teenagers.. She died when she was only 18 years of age.

At 21, I married Jack Harper. Three years later, we were on our way to Malawi, Africa, as missionaries. Those 15 years in Africa were a great blessing to us and we trust we were a blessing to others·too. It is always a privilege to serve the Lord.

"If God calls you to be a missionary, don't stoop to be a king".
(Author unknown.)

J. E. Harper

Uncle Jack — Kirsten's Great Uncle

Some of you are wondering if it is really worthwhile to serve the Lord Jesus faithfully, all your life. You may think that He may ask you to do something in your career that you may not like. However, **God's way and plans are always best for us.**

Since Christ became my Saviour at age thirteen, and I placed my life in His hands, **I have been blessed far beyond whatever I could have planned for myself.**

Whether in University fellowshipping with other Christians, in the Canadian Army Medical Corps, standing at times alone for the Lord, or ministering to young people in Africa with our five children, Jesus has never failed me, nor forsaken me.

Oh, I haven't always been as faithful to Him as I should have been, but now, at almost 80 years of age, I can look back and say, "Thank you Lord Jesus."

"Seek first the Kingdom of God, and His righteousness, and all these things shall be added to you" (Matthew 6:33).

Note to Self

69

Dr. Lee Anne Harper-Femson
Kirsten's Mother

Over my lifetime, I have become increasingly aware of both the brevity and the beauty of life.

The Tsunami that shocked the world in December 2004, followed closely by devastation caused by hurricanes and earthquakes around the world, showed how unpredictable and brief life can be.

On the other hand, hearing about people who have invested time and/or money to assist a community devastated by loss, or hearing about a cure that has been found for some disease, makes me think about the beauty of life and how important it is to reach out and help others in their time of need.

Each morning when I wake up, I trust God to lead me through the day. **I focus on the good things and how I can use every minute to somehow leave a legacy with eternal significance.** As you grow throughout your life, I challenge you to practice the following every day:

Lee Anne with Kirsten and Lauren

Note to Self

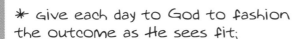

* Give each day to God to fashion the outcome as He sees fit;

* Give meaningful encouragement to someone;

* seek to keep your thoughts wholesome and your motives pure so God can utilize you to do great things for Him;

* treat every chance meeting as a moment where you could influence each person you meet in some positive way;

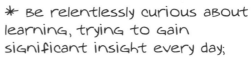

* Be relentlessly curious about learning, trying to gain significant insight every day;

* share your knowledge liberally: what good is knowledge if we don't help someone else with it?

* try to be comfortable with who you are. The sooner you can do that, the more you will develop personally and the more you will enjoy seeing others succeed.

71

Lorie Hartshorn

Director of Development,
Pickering Christian School

Lorie Hartshorn

This passage is my life verse and I
would like to share it with you:

"... Make every effort to add to your faith,
goodness, knowledge, self-control,
perseverance, godliness, brotherly kindness
and love...for if you possess these qualities
in increasing measures, they will keep you
from being ineffective and unproduc-
tive in your knowledge of our Lord
Jesus Christ"
(2 Peter 1:5-11).

As you serve God with all
your heart, I know your
life will be full of many
great adventures ~
Enjoy the ride!

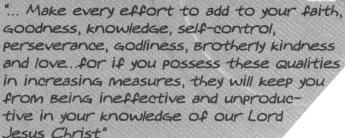

Note to Self

Jeanne W. Hendricks

Author, Friend of Kirsten

The word "wisdom" floats around in our reading and writing like a sparkly gem. Everyone would like to have it, but few of us know how to get it, or even define it, much less wear it. Many ancient writers have called their best ideas wise, and our dictionaries simply call it good sense or discernment. In other words, **wisdom is the ability to find what is best in life and to apply it.** The Bible says that King Solomon was the wisest man who ever lived, so his writings are undoubtedly our best starting place.

In the beginning of Proverbs, Solomon clearly states, *"The fear of the Lord is the beginning of knowledge, but fools despise wisdom and discipline"* (1:7).
This book divides people into four categories:
(1) **simpletons** ~ those who do not or cannot receive wisdom
(2) **fools** ~ those who know it, but ignore it
(3) **mockers** ~ those who know it, but make light of it
(4) **wise** ~ those who receive wisdom and act upon it

Wisdom is more than accumulated knowledge, as Solomon explains to his son. It is recognizing that **no human being has all of the answers to life; therefore, we must diligently seek to cull out the best from our parents and teachers, and to discipline ourselves to make our lives a worthwhile legacy for the next generation. Above all, our fear of the Lord should drive us to please our Creator and to follow His wise principles of living.**

73

Jack Hayford
Senior Pastor, The Church on the Way, Van Nuys, California

I don't have a sermon, but I do have a story. It happened when I was about 11 years old. It was the morning after I'd been at a friend's house ~ a kid named Chuck. The afternoon before we had been goofing around in his room, and he had pulled out a tiny telescope he said his brother had given him. Well, it wasn't a telescope at all. When I peered into it, I saw the crude nude pornographic picture fixed inside. I didn't want to seem out of it, so I laughed, even though inside my chest I felt something like a twinge of pain. (Isn't it funny how much we worry about what people think and we violate trust with our own hearts trying to please someone we'll have so little to do with most of the rest of our lives? I haven't seen Chuck since I went to junior high.)

Anyway, the next day I was about to leave for school when my mama called me into the kitchen. "Jack," she said, "I want to ask you a question. But listen carefully, Son, because I'm asking you in front of Jesus."

I felt as if my heart was about to stop. The few times she ever spoke those words, something real serious was up. I also knew when she said that, I couldn't really

be anything but absolutely truthful ~ no matter what it cost. You see, early in my life, my mom and dad had helped me learn that you can never fake it with God. Looking back, I realize it may be one of the

74

greatest gifts they gave me. Though I was always taught how much God really loves each one of us ~ which is, of course, why He gave us Jesus ~ I also learned His love calls for honesty. As Mama spoke, I sensed I was about to have to face up to truth I would rather avoid. And I was.

"Jack, in front of Jesus, what happened at Chuck's yesterday?" She explained how her heart had felt unexplainably heavy when I had come home the day before. After she had prayed for me and asked Father God why she felt that way, she knew she was to simply ask me about the matter ~ in front of Jesus. Well, I told her what happened and, with sincere tears, asked her to pray with me. My inner sense of uncleanness left, and I was filled with the joyous, conscious, free peace we can all gain in front of Jesus. Minutes later, I was on my way to school, relieved of a huge weight that had been lifted off my chest.

So, that's it ~ the memory I felt pretty sure you'd be interested to hear. I thought you'd like the story behind a great life-secret (my mother) taught me. In short, it's that **life is a lot more fulfilling and the heart is freer to be and keep happy, when we remain open and aboveboard with Christ. Life really works only when we shoot straight with God.**

Abridged excerpt:
"From a Father's Heart" by Jack Hayford.

Note to Self

Kurt Kaiser
Composer, Musician

KURT KAISER MUSIC, INC.
4910 BROOKS DRIVE
WACO, TEXAS 76710
254.776.2699   kkaiser@flash.net

I have been thinking about this thing called wisdom.
Wisdom is difficult to analyze. I had a very good friend,
the principal cellist of the Dallas Symphony, who seemed
to know everything! World religions, music, political
systems, art, philosophy, people ~ he knew so much. We
had lunch together monthly and I often wondered
where his wisdom came from. It came from respect
for others; it came from life experiences, including
prison camps; it came from an inquisitiveness to learn;
it came from listening. Wisdom comes with maturity.

The Bible has many references to wisdom. For example,
Proverbs 9:10 states, "The fear of God is the
beginning of wisdom." **Wisdom could be compared to
the Christian's life. It is a continual pilgrimage of
growth and not a one
time epiphany.**

Note to Self

Dr. Norman Kee
Physician, Orillia, Ontario

I have just celebrated 38 years of serving as a family physician. I can't think of anything I would rather do. To be taken into a person's trust is truly a humbling experience.

Out of those years of interacting with hundreds if not thousands of people, during times of joy and sorrow, elation and heart break, a few nuggets of wisdom have emerged.

First, there is more to life than work and a corollary to that, there is more to work than making money. When I keep those two thoughts before me on a daily basis, I become less stressed and a more happy and fulfilled individual. Try it! It works!

Second, most of what upsets me will have little or no effect on me even in as little as one week's time. So why not apply the "five year rule". If whatever is "stressing me out" to-day will not be of any significance to me five years from now, I am going to choose to not let it upset me to-day. There are things that will continue to impact me on a long term basis. Those are the issues that I will concentrate on.

77

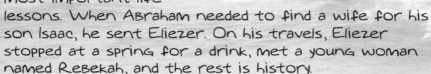

Sue Kline
Editor of Discipleship Journal

A servant named Eliezer taught me one of my most important life lessons. When Abraham needed to find a wife for his son Isaac, he sent Eliezer. On his travels, Eliezer stopped at a spring for a drink, met a young woman named Rebekah, and the rest is history.

Hidden in this story is the gem that has helped to shape my life. For Eliezer summed up his quest this way: "I being in the way, the Lord led me" (Genesis 24:27).

Life is a series of decisions. Sometimes it gets scary: What if I choose the wrong path? Eliezer's words have helped me move toward even the toughest decisions with confidence that **if I stay "in the way," intimate with God, then He will show me what to do.**

Let God speak to you through the book He wrote, the Bible. Talk to Him through prayer. And while you're talking in prayer, don't forget to listen: He still speaks today, Spirit to spirit. Let His whisper to your spirit be your guide to life's decisions.

Note to Self

The Hon. C. Everett Koop

Former Surgeon-General of the U.S.A.

Our faith as Christians is based on promises, not feelings. We have the assurance that God's son, Jesus loved us enough to die for us. If he would do that, is there anything he would withhold from you, except to protect you from harm?

Everything that God does for you is for your good, no matter how you "feel" about it. The only thing that can separate you from God's love is sin (anything less than God's perfection) ~ But if you believe what I've written above, God has already forgiven your sin, past, present, and future. Your life in eternity with Him is guaranteed.

As Horatio Spafford* wrote in his great hymn, "My sin, not in part, but the whole, is nailed to the cross, and I bear it no more: Praise the Lord, praise the Lord, O my soul!"

*Horatio Gates Spafford wrote the words for this hymn He lived from 1828-1888. Great Hymns of the Faith. Compiled by and edited by John W. Peterson, (1968) Michigan: Singspiration Music. p. 256.

Dr. Woodrow Kroll
President, Back to the Bible International

Solomon was the wisest man who ever lived. He wanted to pass on to his children some of the wisdom his father David passed on to him. That's why he wrote the Book of Proverbs in the Bible.

His purpose for writing (Proverbs 1:2-6) was: to help us attain disciplined wisdom, insightful understanding, acquire a disciplined life, learn what is right, just and fair, avoid being spiritually naïve, learn discretion when we are young, add to the learning we already have, get discerning guidance, and to understand the proverbs, parables, sayings and riddles of his book.

Solomon distinguished between simple knowledge and true wisdom. Knowledge is what you learn relating to facts, figures, stories, etc. Wisdom is the skill to use your knowledge in the right way. Wisdom only comes from God. There's no other place to get it. "For the Lord gives wisdom" (Proverbs 2:6).

Note to Self

You can get knowledge without wisdom, but for your education to be complete, you need to learn how to filter everything you learn through the wisdom of God's Word.

Dr. Matti Leisola

Professor, D.Sc. (Tech.), Dean of the Faculty of Chemical
Technology, Helsinki University of Technology

I have been doing science for more than thirty years.
Modern science was born in a Christian world with
great Christian thinkers like Faraday and Maxwell. Since
these days science has changed to a totalitarian
naturalistic religion which tries to be the universal
method of finding truth about nature and humans.

I do not believe that humans evolved from animals but
were created as an image of God. This gives a true
basis for human dignity, morals and ethics. This gives us a
reason to value human life from conception to the very
last breath. Man is also a fallen sinner. This explains the
problems we face in our world.

This life is finally a short moment and can be compared
to a train station where people are waiting for a train
which takes them to eternity. Be sure to be on the
right train.

I like the words of Martin Luther concerning Jesus: "I
am the Way and the Truth and the Life... hold me tightly
with faith and full confidence; I am the bridge and shall
carry you to the other side so that in a moment you will
be transferred from death and fear of Hell to that life.

I have made that way and walked it
myself so that I can carry everyone
who hangs to me to the other side.
Hang without doubt and worry gladly
to me and die bravely trusting in me."

81

Kirsten

Michele Lopers
Teacher, Kirsten's Synchronized Swimming Coach

We can be sure of one thing. God created us for a purpose. He gives you gifts and talents to be used in service for Him. He tells us in Jeremiah 29:11 "For I know the plans I have for you declares the Lord, plans to prosper you and not to harm you, plans to give you hope and a future" (Jeremiah 29:11 NIV).

Invite God into your heart. Rely on his guidance and trust Him. Ask God for the wisdom to discern His plan for your life. Bring Him to school with you. Ask for His guidance when choosing courses, friends and activities.

When choosing a career, choose something that you are good at and enjoy. When we use our gifts in service to Him, we are building up His kingdom. God would want you to enjoy the work you are called to do! He loves you.

Finally, don't be lazy. Your life, everyday, is a gift from God. What you become is your gift to Him.

Rev. Norm MacLaren
Vice-President, Crossroads Family of Ministries

For some, learning is the greatest goal of life, but knowledge without wisdom is like an empty drum. It is a great container but lacks substance. In the Bible, there is a book called Ecclesiastes. Chapter 1 verse 18 says "for in much wisdom is much grief, and he who increases knowledge increases sorrow." Knowledge and wisdom in and of themselves are of little value. Together they can enfold science, accumulate wealth, even bring power and position, but they do not bring inner peace of soul and heart.

In Ecclesiastes chapter 12:1 it says "Remember now your Creator in the days of your youth, Before the difficult days come, And the years draw near when you say, 'I have no pleasure in them.'" Now, while you are young is the time to allow God to show you His way, that when you are old you will not be bitter over wasted years and much sorrow. Wisdom and knowledge together are of vast value, but wisdom and knowledge directed by our Lord is priceless.

Note to Self

83

David Mainse

Founder of CCCI and Former Host
of "100 Huntley Street"

**Are your goals "GOD CENTRED"
or "SELF CENTRED?"**

David
Mainse.

The most
"GOD
CENTRED"
person in the entire universe said,
*"NOT MY WILL BUT YOURS BE
DONE."* (Matthew 26:39B)

The most "SELF-CENTRED"
person in the universe said, *"I WILL"*
five times in one sentence.
(Isaiah 14:13-14)

How will you choose to live?

Jesus said, *"IF ANYONE
DESIRES TO COME
AFTER ME, LET HIM
DENY HIMSELF AND
TAKE UP HIS CROSS
DAILY AND FOLLOW
ME."* (Matthew 16:24).

Note to Self

Norma-Jean Mainse

Recording Artist, Crossroads / 100 Huntley Street

The greatest advice I could ever give to a student is the word of God. The Bible is full of great wisdom. I would strongly advise you to read the Book of Proverbs. Some of my favorite scripture verses are... for guidance Proverbs 3:5 & 6, "Trust in the Lord with all your heart, and lean not on your own understanding; In all your ways acknowledge Him and He shall direct your paths."

Norma-Jean Mainse

A great verse regarding your future is... "For I know the thoughts that I think toward you, says the Lord, thoughts of peace and not of evil, to give you a future and a hope. The you will call upon Me and go and pray to Me, and I will listen to you. And you will seek Me and find Me, when you search for Me with all your heart." (Jeremiah 29:11-13).

If you will put God first in your life, you will see Him do great and mighty things in your life. God will always be there for us, however, the onus is on us to SEEK HIM... Ephesians 6:10-11, "Finally, my brethren, (students) be strong in the Lord and in the power of His might. Put on the whole armor of God, that you may be able to stand against the wiles of the devil."

Remember, "I can do all things through Christ who strengthens me" (Philippians 4:13). Let the beauty of Jesus, His love and compassion be seen in your life. Your life may be the only Bible some people will ever read.

85

Reynold and Kathy Mainse

T.V. Hosts, Humanitarian Aid Workers

Be passionate... about what?
Stuff? No. Others? Yes!

A life lived for personal gain, though busy, often ends lonely. A life shared with and lived for others can never be counted as wasted. It is a life of joy and some-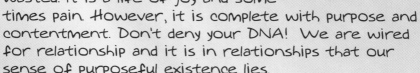

Reynold & Kathy Mainse

times pain. However, it is complete with purpose and contentment. Don't deny your DNA! We are wired for relationship and it is in relationships that our sense of purposeful existence lies.

Our message is one of passion and compassion. Jesus Christ gave us the greatest example of this. He loved us all so much (passion) that He gave His life (compassion) so that we might be brought back into right relationship with God.

Note to Self

When you embrace the reality of God's passionate love for you, you'll feel compelled and find it completely fulfilling to live a life of passion that is fuelled by compassion. This is the kind of life that will change our world!

Ron and Ann Mainse

Hosts of "100 Huntley Street",
Crossroads Family of Ministries

"You have your whole life ahead of you!"
"These are the best days of your life!" "If I
would've known then what I know now..." It
seems the older we get, the more clichés
we hear. Good advice that never grows
old. Or does it? Sometimes too much good
advice can begin to have just the opposite
effect and make us callous to its simple
truth, causing us to miss out on some
pretty good words of wisdom. During this
"bursting at the seams with possibilities"
time in your life...that time when you're
ready to "hit the ground running' into all
the future holds, remember one thing:
remember to not only "stop and smell the
roses" but maybe more importantly, take a
few of them with you on your journey.
For there's a lot to be said for "the
wisdom of the ages" from those who have
traveled the path already.

Ron & Ann
Mainse

And if we could leave you
with one small rose for
the road...Remember,
you're never alone. If you
let Him, God will lead you
on the greatest
adventure of your life.
You've only just begun!

87

Agnes McKechnie
Friend of Kirsten's Grandma

Encouragement. We all need it! The Bible tells us to "encourage one another and build each other up" (IThessalonians 5:11). There is a sad lack of encouragement today. "We live by encouragement and we die without it-slowly, sadly and angrily." (Celeste Holme) "How many people stop because so few say 'Go'?" (Charles Swindoll)

Each of us can give meaningful encouragement. Opportunities abound if we are sensitively aware of others and realize the uplifting effect it has to brighten a person's day. **Words aptly spoken or simple acts of kindness can give inspiration and confidence to a disheartened, anxious soul.**

There is no greater encouragement for us than in the words of the Lord Himself. *"The King will reply, 'I tell you the truth, whatever you did for one of the least of these brothers of mine, you did for me."* (Matthew 25:40).

Never miss an opportunity to revive a person's hope and spirit. Why withhold it?

Note to Self

88

Dr. Francis Mpindu

Pastor, College Professor, Police Chaplain.

Dr. Francis Mpindu

Think about education as a PRIVILEGE! In our present day of elevating our rights, you need to look at education differently if you are to appreciate the education system.

I was raised in a country where some children never went to school simply because the parents could not afford it or because their parents saw no value in formal education. Therefore, I count it a great honor and privilege to have gone to school, both in my native country (Zimbabwe), Kenya, South Africa, and here in Canada. My background has helped me to appreciate life as a gift from God. Now, I look back and marvel at God's grace in my life. **The world does not owe me anything. Instead, I owe everything to God.**

Someone said, "True education is what you remain with after you forget all they taught you in school."

School is cool, man!

I encourage you to view education as a process rather than an achievement. This process takes place as four God given institutions work hand-in-hand in educating children to be responsible citizens of Canada and heaven. The four institutions are the Government, the Church, the Home, and the School. May your formal education process assist you to integrate all the life skills you learn from these God-given institutions.

Dr. John M. Moore

International Evangelist, Songwriter

Go After Wisdom!

Solomon, the son of King David, became the wisest man on the face of the earth. People travelled from all over the world to listen to him. We may trace his wisdom to a most important choice he made while still a young man. The Bible tells us that one night God appeared to Solomon at the beginning of his reign as the king of Israel, and said to him ~ "Ask! What shall I give you!" (2 Chronicles 1:7).

Solomon did not ask for wealth, or for honor, or for the destruction of all his enemies, or for a long life, his request was simply: "Give me wisdom and knowledge!" (2 Chronicles 1:10). His humble request was granted, and since he did not ask for these other blessings, God was happy to include them.

Note to Self

James, the brother of Jesus, said: "If any of you lacks wisdom, let him ask of God, who gives to all liberally and without reproach, and it will be given to him." Dr. Vance Havner wrote: "If you lack knowledge, go to school. If you lack wisdom, get on your knees. Knowledge is not wisdom. Wisdom is the proper use of knowledge."

The apostle Paul said, "Christ is the power of God and the wisdom of God." (I Corinthians 1:24). So, in order to receive the wisdom that comes from above, we must be sure that we have a personal relationship with God through Jesus Christ. We begin by receiving Jesus Christ, the Son of God, as our personal Lord and Saviour in an act of faith and repentance, and we confess to others our allegiance to Him.

"For to know God, and Jesus Christ whom He has sent, is the highest principle and perfection of man. This attainment, infinitely above all others, constitutes true wisdom." (Charles Simeon).

GO AFTER WISDOM!

91

Bill Myers
Author

Many people say they are Christian. They may go to church, they may pray, they may even read their Bible on a regular basis. All of these things are important. But **it is only the Christian who agrees to say YES to God at all times who will have the abundant overflowing life that Jesus promises us in John 10:10.** The Christian who will say:

Yes!!!!!

Yes when it doesn't make sense.
Yes when we're sure God has made a mistake.
Yes when we're sure we're unqualified.
Yes when it's frightening.
Yes when we know many more people are far better equipped.

God does not need great men and women. Most of the Bible's heroes were losers at one time or another. You do not need to be smart, you do not need to be clever, you do not need to be talented, you don't even have to be particularly "holy." **All you need do is be willing to say yes.** There are so few of those in the Body of Christ willing to do this that the Lord has to use whoever He can get. Even me. Even you.

Note to Self

Bill Nickerson

Femson Family Friend

Be very careful from whom you take advice. Counsel from the wise around us is a gift for our safety. Proverbs 11:14 says *there is "safety in many counselors."* Try not to be hurried in your life decisions, especially the many large decisions you will be making that affect you long-term. Look and listen for the Lord's leading and voice.

Many a time I've been saved by wise counsel of others and often I've suffered for not seeking nor heeding sound advice.

God is FOR us, seek Him first. Rich is the person who has a good relationship with Him and better early in life. You were created for fellowship with God, created for awesome creativity and ability, develop it all well. Be prayerfully daring in the Lord and His might.

Treat everyone with dignity and respect. Remember how Jesus treated people.

Finally, run a good race. It is a marathon, with a few sprints thrown in. Run in faith looking to Jesus.

93

Kirsten and
Paul Ogborne

Paul Ogborne

Teacher, Principal, Pickering Christian School

"I will lift up my eyes to the mountains from whence shall my help come? My help comes from the Lord who made heaven and earth" (Psalm 121: 1-2).

Look up...work hard...finish well.

In whatever activity or situation you find yourself, remember these six words. **Look** to the Lord for direction and strength, do your **best** all the time and complete your tasks as one who is grateful of the life God has given you.

Note to Self

Dr. James I. Packer

Professor of Theology, Regent College, Vancouver
Author of "Knowing God"

Dr Packer

All through your life, along every road, round
every corner, in every situation and
relationship, when on your own and when in company,
**never forget that your best friend is always with you.
Who is that? Jesus**, your sin-bearing Saviour, your
Teacher and your Boss. Talk to him every day about the
day. Be sure of his love for you. Trust him for protection and help and aim to please him in all you do, even
if that means displeasing people who are trying to lead
you away from him.

**Never forget that your worst enemy is with you too,
every day of your life. Who is that? Satan,** the
Adversary (that is what his name means), who wishes
you harm because he wishes God harm, and tries to
spoil everything that God does. Once you become a
believer, God goes to work on you to make you Jesus-
like and Satan tries to spoil and block God's work by
making you rebellious and Satan-like. **Be on guard, and
keep asking the Lord Jesus
to direct you through
Scripture and the Holy Spirit
to keep you from falling
into Satan's traps.**

As we say to each other
every day, more wisely perhaps
than we know ~ take care!

Dr. Luis Palau

Author, President, Luis Palau Associates

"The primary purpose of the Bible is not to tell us how the heavens go, but how to go to heaven. **The Bible's great message is that God desires to transform the lives of His children through His Word, preparing them for eternity with Him in glory.**"

Excerpt from Palau, L. (1994) "Healthy Habits for Spiritual Growth." Michigan: Discovery House Publishers, p.33.
Reprinted with permission, permission granted, September 22, 2005.

John W. Peterson

Composer, Publisher, John W. Peterson Music Company

In the pursuit of your dreams be prepared for some disappointments ~ they will come. But do not let them discourage or deter you. **Be resilient. Bounce back... press on!** I am ashamed to tell you how many rejection letters I received before my first song was accepted and published.

Also, it is vital that you make room in your schedule for being alone with the Lord ~ to talk to Him and read His Word. It is in such "quiet times," as they are called by some, that God is enabled to give you direction and provide grace and strength to live a dynamic, successful Christian life. When, where or how long you set aside to do this is not as important as being consistent.

Note to Self

97

Don Palmer
Senior Pastor, Forest Brook Bible Chapel

What is wisdom? Today, we often associate it with being intelligent or smart. But when the Bible talks about wisdom, it means a skill or ability to think the right way and then to do the right thing. Therefore wisdom is very practical, is a gift from God and is not natural to us. It helps us see things how God sees them and involves our whole lifestyle, including everything we think, say and do. Without wisdom, nothing in life will make sense ~ no matter how clever we become.

The starting point for receiving wisdom from God is in learning to "fear" him ~ this means to respect, reverence and keep God in awe. Today we would describe this as a having a relationship with God, worshipping him and submitting to his will in everything we do. We receive wisdom from God when we admit we need it, ask him for it and then use it in all the big and small decisions we have to make everyday.

In the Old Testament in particular, **the Bible portrays two "ways" or paths: the way of the wise and the way of the fool.** The way of the wise leads to greater understanding from God and is described as the "right way", a "straight way" and the "way of life". Contrary to this is the way of the fool, which often seems right in our eyes, but in reality is "wicked", "hard", "deceitful" and "leads to death"!

Apart from some of the Psalms, there are four books of the Bible which are regarded as "wisdom books" (Proverbs, Song of Solomon, Ecclesiastes and Job). In these four books we learn how we need wisdom in the following ways: (a) in all the various decisions we need to make everyday (Proverbs); (b) in the relationship between a man and a woman (Song of Solomon, or Songs of songs); (c) in trying to understand the meaning of life (Ecclesiastes) and (d) in trying to understand why people suffer (Job). Solomon was regarded as the wisest person who ever lived. He is reported to have spoken over 3000 proverbs (ie. wise sayings).

Note to Self

Probably, the most famous Proverb (wise saying) is recorded in Proverbs 3:5-6 and says "Trust in the LORD with all your heart and lean not on your own understanding; in all your ways acknowledge him, and he will make your paths straight."

Kevin Pauls
Music Ministry

Kirsten Femson
and Kevin Pauls

Dream BiG!! Dream Often!!

Many want to suggest that life is not about dreams, but about settling for what you can achieve. Reality has a way of stealing your youthful dreams. Do not allow yourself to listen to those who say you can't do something. Your reality does not have to be the same as everyone else's. **Dreams are not there to torment you. They are there to motivate you to achieve them. Dreams are often God's blueprint for your life.**

I dare you to dream BIG! And dream OFTEN!!

Tom Potterfield
Author, teacher, Businessman

"Think deeply, discover what you love, and never lose sight of the fact that things can be different."

I wrote the above when dedicating my first book to my daughter, Kate. I meant it as a prescriptive to counter the shallowness, conformity, and apathy that characterizes much of our contemporary society. In my life, I have encountered many people (including me!!!) who were unable to grasp what really creates passion within us. Too often, we become what others expect or advise us to become. We too easily believe that the way things are is somehow the way they should or must be. This results in a shrunken sense of self and the bland perpetuation of a culture that treasures only economic values, that sees humans instrumentally--as a market or a resource to be exploited, and that attempts to prescribe material gratification as the answer to questions of meaning and significance.

Go deeper. **Be aware of what feeds your soul and brings you joy.** Know that the dictates and characteristics of our economy, our society, our politics are human constructions and can thus be altered by concerned, active citizens. We can help to bring the Kingdom to our earthly existence and create social, economic and political arrangements that take greater heed of human need. We can help change this crazy world.

Paul Pryce
Street Youth Specialist

Remember that when life comes to an end, it matters not what you take with you, But what you leave Behind. Wealth, fame and power have no effect when this life is over. **What matters is the legacy of life you leave Behind. What difference will you make in the lives of others?** People will remember the love you showed to those less fortunate than yourselves, they will marvel at the life lived with integrity and they will rejoice in the accomplishments that you have made, that improve the life of others. By no means should we strive to Be average, But **we should focus our energies on using wisely the gifts God has given each of us to accomplish His will.** When we work towards His will, a new measure of greatness can be achieved, one that will long outlast any benefits we might achieve through wealth, fame and power. **The power to change this world and make an impact on those around you comes from knowing God and seeking His will in your life.** You are the future of this country, its time to make it a Better place to live.

Note to Self

Kirsten Femson with Charles Price

Charles Price
Pastor, Teacher, The Peoples Church

How you do things is more important than what you do.

For instance, it is right that we have possessions we call our own, but it is wrong to steal to get them. So a right thing can be obtained in a wrong way, and the way you get them is more important than the thing itself.

It is right we have friends, but if we try to build a friendship with a person we like by being nasty to someone else who also wants their friendship, we are trying to get a right thing in a wrong way. It is right to want to win a race, but if you cheat and stop someone else from winning who is faster than you, you are trying to get a right thing in a wrong way.

It is not the things we do and accomplish that is the most important thing about us, it is the kind of person we are, which means, it is the way we do those things. What we do changes from day to day, but the kind of person we are stays the same whatever we are doing.

This is why Jesus said, 'Seek first the kingdom of God and His righteousness and everything else will be given to you'. We only get ourselves right when we realize we can't change ourselves by ourselves ~

Peoples
CHURCH TORONTO
Services
Sunday at 9:15, 11:30 am & 6:00pm

374 Sheppard Avenue East
www.thepeopleschurch.ca

we need God to change us by living in us and producing His character in us.

In eighty years from now, when your grandchildren and great-grandchildren talk about you, they will not talk so much about what you do or did, but the kind of person you are or were. The kind of grandparent you become depends on the kind of parent you become, and the kind of parent you become depends on the kind of adult you become, and the kind of adult you become depends on the kind of person you are now, and the kind of person you are now depends on who is in charge of your life. Is it Jesus, with all strength, love and kindness, that leads and strengthens you, or is it just you?

That is the biggest question you will have to answer in your life ~ and most of us have to answer it while we are young.

Note to Self

Chris Quinn

Business Administrator,
Pickering Christian School, 2003

"The joy of the LORD is your strength"
(Nehemiah 8:10).

I urge all of you to allow God to grow His Joy, His
Passion and His Faithfulness in you as you mature in
Christ. Continue to fly His Banner over your lives — Be
faithful to the hope that is in you and God will direct
your paths and make His face to shine upon you.

Note to Self

Marion I. Roberts
Kirsten's Piano Teacher

Make a difference!

You are now faced with choices that will affect the rest of your life. Challenge this new life in small steps. Do not be afraid to push yourself to learn and grow. With an idea, determination and the right tools you can do great things.

No one else can live your life. When making choices, use all your talents, instincts, and your heart to guide you, despite all the bad things happening around us ~ war, hunger, poverty and terrorism. Being a super hero isn't the thing. Know and be who you really are. There is only one you, and you will pass this particular way only once.

Look around you. Believe in the incredible power of the human mind, of working hard, of laughing and hoping.

Reach out and make a difference.

"Two roads diverged in a wood and I ~ I took the one less traveled, and that has made all the difference."

Robert Frost

Ginger H. Robinson

President, FACE the Challenge, Centennial, Colorado

Ginger Robinson

Since our surgical teams first performed free facial surgeries in 1993, my best reckoning is that 873 indigent patients have received life-changing surgeries by August 2005. I am profoundly moved that Our Father has chosen to show His favor in this way. My facial surgeon husband, Randolph (Randy) C. Robinson, MD, DDS and I share a common mission. Our organization, FACE the Challenge, aims to show the compassion of Christ by providing surgeries mostly for children, but also adults, in developing countries. Repeatedly, we are gratified when these patients can face their futures with more hope.

When I was 14, I felt a desire to serve the Lord through a medical ministry. Who put this desire in my heart? I believe it was God Himself. **What has God placed on your heart? How has He uniquely gifted you? As none of us may know for certain what the will of God is as we are young, be assured that as you trust in Him, He will be faithful in His guidance.**

Be patient with how He might be at work in your life. It took over 20 years for my dream to become a reality. Perhaps His plan will be revealed through circumstances, your choices to move ~ perhaps initially with small, uncertain steps in a general direction and wise counsel of others. Be still, watchful, and alert for how He might be directing you. Recognize, too, that there will be unexpected turns along the way. Accept that and try to be flexible, trusting Him the more.

As I have advised our three children who also face decisions that impact their lives, I would say the same for you. In all that is happening in your life, "Be joyful in hope, patient in affliction, and faithful in prayer" Romans 12:12 (NIV). So much of what I have done, believing that it is according to His will, has occurred behind the scenes and at times during much affliction.

At times I ask, "What are my goals?" I ponder, "Are they to achieve the praise of humans?" Or, "Is it to be found faithful as His servant-child?" As Charles Haddon Spurgeon has reminded me, especially when I have struggled as a wife, mother, nurse, and president of a relief organization: "Be content to live unknown for a little while and walk your weary way through the fields of poverty or up the hills of affliction; for soon enough you will reign with Christ."

Whatever your call is, God will honor your faithful, passionate, and loving service to His children. Your reward is in Heaven, not here. Believe it and continue on.

Note to Self

Note to Self

ADRIAN ROGERS
Pastor Emeritus

BELLEVUE BAPTIST CHURCH
Memphis, Tennessee

Dr. Adrian Rogers
Pastor Emeritus, Bellevue Baptist Church, Memphis.

I have observed that **the earlier a student sets his or her course in life, the more likely success will be his or hers.**

The purpose of life is to find, to follow, and to finish the will of God for one's life. Students should sign their name on the bottom of a piece of blank paper, and let God fill it in I am speaking figuratively, but that needs to be done in the heart and mind of each person.

Every student needs to consider what true success is. One definition of failure is succeeding at the wrong thing. Ask yourself this question, and ask it sincerely and honestly: If I get to where I am headed, where will I be?

Luella G. Rolfe
80-year-old Friend of Kirsten

What an honor, as an 80-year-old, to be asked for wisdom!

Never go to bed angry.

Be careful of what you say, it could come back to you!

Ask yourself: what kind of Church would there be if everyone was like me?

Seek home for rest, for home is best.

Do unto others as you would have others do unto you.

Live a good Christian life. Trust God in all things ~ Sometimes He closes a door, but be patient He may open two.

In time of loss ~ be better not bitter!

Find a job you like and you will never work a day in your life.

Lindy Ruff
Head Coach (Buffalo Sabres)

You gain wisdom from all of your peers as you go through life. The people I gained most of my wisdom through were my parents. They gave me the base of knowledge to make the best decisions. The teachers that taught me through school were also a great example for me. They taught me the values of doing well in school and that the work you put in will eventually help you when you become an adult. Wisdom came from a lot of my teammates as I went through my sports career. They were great examples of how to compete at the highest level. They also taught me how to be a good example for younger people.

I have also gained wisdom from the mistakes I made, learning to make better decisions next time. Life is full of adventure! Pick a good role model and let your parents help you along the way.

Note to Self

112

Dr. Michael E. Schmidt

Speaker, Professional Trumpet Player

Shortly after my Grandmother "Nana" passed away, members of my family could hardly wait to open a small secretary desk where Nana was said to have kept her most "valuable" things. Hastily Nana's desk was opened before we could even find the key. Little did we know that what we would find in Nana's desk were tokens themselves. For almost a century, Nana had saved all of the cards, letters, pictures, notes, newspaper clippings, church bulletins and sermons that people had given to her.

The priceless treasure that our family found in Nana's desk was **the three greatest jewels in life; evidence of her faith, her family and friends.** It is my prayer that each and every one of you will be inspired to utilize the priceless treasure that was found in Nana's little desk.

113

Dr. Judith Shamian
President of V.O.N. Canada

Kirsten wit
Dr. Shamiar

In the past 30 years of my work as a nurse (Chief Nurse of Canada for five years), a researcher, a teacher, a leader and as the President/CEO of the Victorian Order of Nurses for Canada, I learned some very important lessons about people. My work has allowed me to travel and work with people in every continent. I am lucky to have done it as a nurse because people trust nurses and talk to nurses.

In my travels, I have learned one really important thing. **People everywhere, of every size, shape, colour and religion, are all looking for the same thing — to belong, to be heard, and to matter.** We might look different, sound different, wear different clothes and go to different schools and churches, but, whether we live in Canada, Tibet, Somalia or Peru, we really are all very similar. **We all have something to contribute.**

My challenges to you? **Work hard in school and whatever you do in life. It really does make a difference in the end, even if it feels hard today.** Try to be positive. Be good to people, and look for the best in them. If you live your life that way, I promise you, all good things will come back to you.

Dr. Charles F. Stanley

Senior Pastor, NY Times Best-selling author,
Founder and President of In Touch Ministries

I believe the most important lesson I have ever learned is ~ **obey God and leave all the consequences to Him.**

To be obedient to God and leave the consequences to Him requires two things: Number one, it requires that you learn how to listen to God. If you do not know how to listen to God to find His will for your life, then you will not know how to be obedient to Him. That's why you cannot separate learning to listen from obedience.

A second thing that is absolutely essential to obedience is that you trust Him. Since God is under no obligation to show you the consequences ahead of time, then you have to guard your heart against fear. Remember Romans 8:28 when fear of the future tries to hinder your faith and trust in Him.

Never forget that God is responsible for the consequences of your obedience. It is your responsibility to learn how to listen to Him and your responsibility to trust Him. God will never fail to take care of one of His children who trust in His heart of love.

Note to Self

115

Dr. Brian Stiller

President, Tyndale University College & Seminary

Dr. Brian Stiller.

Let your dreams shape your hopes. Dreams, of what we'd like to do and become, pop up without our planning or engineering. Poof: they are there.

Nurture those dreams, for they rise from the very stuff of your being.

Your life is not the result of a haphazard, chance encounter of an egg and sperm. You are always in the mind of the Creator. That's why your dreams make sense, for they speak of who you are.

Be careful though. Those dreams can too easily be robbed. Protect them. Nurture them into your hopes, the architectural framework for who you will become.

We don't automatically become who we'll be. That comes by the choices and disciplines of our own choosing. So in your dreams and hopes, choose wisely.

Note to Self

116

John Storm

Author, Speaker, Father, Son, Husband, Fisherman, Seeker, Joker, Teacher, Student, Learner, Christian, Friend, Human, BoxPerson

When I think about important things I've learned so far in this life, things I wish I'd known as a teenager, things I'm still learning ... it might be summed up in one word ... BOXES!

Life is full of boxes. Not just the physical boxes that we ship, store, protect, and fill with our "stuff". Life is also full of "boxes" ~ mental models, premises, and paradigms ~ that affect the way we see ourselves, other people, and the world all around us.

It's easy to put other people in boxes based on just a tiny bit of what we see on the outside. It's easy for other people to put us in boxes, too. Yet, rarely can we accurately describe a person with just a few simple labels. Being a living, breathing human being defies definition! One of the amazing things about human beings is that we are very complex. There are a LOT of things going on inside our minds.

Note to Self

Which is why... **it's so important for us to identify, evaluate, and modify the boxes we discover.**

I've learned there are 3 kinds of boxes in life:

1. Boxes we crawl into by the decisions we make

2. Boxes others put us in based on what they see or experience

3. Boxes that Life just delivers to us (good boxes and bad ones)

I hope you will take some time to think about the boxes you find yourself in and the boxes you put other people in.

Perhaps you'll find a few that need to be opened and re-evaluated. Some may be worth hanging on to, others may need to be changed, and maybe a few will need to be thrown in the trash.

Be assured, God loves you and cares about you and your boxes. Ask Him for the wisdom to select those that contain the good things in life. May you discover the gifts of peace, joy, and love along the way.

Dr. John Stott
Author, Founder, Langham Partnership

Our teen years are a good time to commit our lives to Christ. I was in Grade 11 when I heard Christ knocking at the door of my heart and opened the door to Him. Now I am 84-years-old, so I have had 67 years in which to follow and serve Jesus Christ.

I hope and pray that you will do the same.

11-AUG-2005 16:53   FROM:JOHN STOTT 02075804335   TO:001905A203895

from **John Stott**
office address **12 Weymouth Street London W1W 5BY**

TEL: 020 7580 1867 (Int. +44 20 7580 1867)   FAX: 020 7580 4335 (Int +44 20 7580 4335)

August 2005

Our teen years are a good time to commit our lives to Christ. I was in Grade 11 when I heard Christ knocking at the door of my heart and opened the door to him. Now I am 84 years old, so that I have had 67 years in which to follow and serve Jesus Christ. I hope and pray that you will do the same.

John Stott.

120

Jean Stratmeyer

Missionary

I believe Christians are to be "salt and light". As our lives reflect truth, honesty, helpfulness, respect and productive work, they are a testimony of the truths of Scripture, of salvation and Christian growth.

For those who enter missionary work, we need, as Christians, to share the Gospel, without insisting on the assimilation of Western culture. Nationals must be encouraged to cultivate those things which are wholesome in their own cultural patterns, especially in relationship to music and worship.

Because of the work of missionaries in establishing clinics, schools, seminaries and Bible Schools, many national children now have an opportunity to receive an education. Many go on to become teachers, government workers, mechanics or whatever they are led to pursue. The Gospel is bringing a greater sense of worth and dignity to these people.

Recognize and take advantage of the many opportunities you have to influence your culture and others for the Lord. But remember, **a subtle influence is often more effective than a dogmatic influence.**

Note to Self

Note to Self

Lucile Sugden
Teacher

Put God first in your life and ask Jesus to guide you in finding a career that you will enjoy and that is God's will.

We are to love the Lord Jesus and love one another. Never let discouragement and hate enter your life. The Holy Spirit is in you & let Him fill your life.

Love & obey your parents. **When you start working, do a little more than is expected of you.**

Joni

Joni Eareckson Tada

Author, Artist, Speaker

When I broke my neck, I experienced some of the same struggles, problems, hopes and dreams that you do. Little did I realize that God would deal with me in such a traumatic way. Probably most of you haven't had an accident like mine, but there's no doubt you see lots of similarities between the troubles I faced and the sort of things you are going through now.

The one message I'd like to get across more than any other is that of God's enormous love for each one of us. **He cares so much about every detail of our lives and how we feel about ourselves.** He wants us to have a good self-image and to see our worth and dignity through His eyes. He paid an enormous price to show us how valuable we are to Him.

May you keep near to the Lord as you grow in Him more and more each day. And may you **seek out opportunities to reach out to people who are disabled all around you, through your church, a** local nursing home, or a rehabilitation hospital.

123

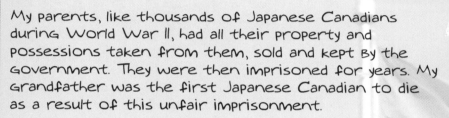

David Tsubou

The Hon. David Tsubouchi
Chair of Management Board of Cabinet
and Minister of Culture

This year I received the Bryden Award for Leadership from York University. In my acceptance speech, I spoke about my role models — my parents.

My parents, like thousands of Japanese Canadians during World War II, had all their property and possessions taken from them, sold and kept by the government. They were then imprisoned for years. My grandfather was the first Japanese Canadian to die as a result of this unfair imprisonment.

In August 1944, Prime Minister MacKenzie King declared that no person of the Japanese race had ever been charged with disloyalty.

My mother died prematurely as a result of an illness she contracted while imprisoned. They both lost the best years of their lives behind barbed wire.

My father is not bitter. He believes strongly in Canada despite his hardship. My parents, like your parents, only want a better life for you. Your parents are the best role models that you can have.

Do not let the past be a tyrant to your lives. Look to the future with optimism but remember the lessons of the past.

Message to the Pickering Christian School Graduating Class, 2003

Marlene Waters
Friend of Kirsten

As a Christian, you know that the Lord promises to be with you, to never leave you or forsake you. I once had a wise person share with me, "God does not see you as you are at this very moment. He already sees you, standing before His throne in Heaven. God knows your every path. He sees you as you will be, having completed your life."

Long ago, even before He made the world, God chose us to be His very own. He decided then to make us holy in His eyes, without a single fault ~ we who stand before Him covered with His love. **You do not need to worry about your tomorrows, for Christ has already been there.**

Remember the words of the Apostle Paul: *"I pray that your hearts will be flooded with light so that you can see something of the future He has called you to share ~ that you will begin to understand how great is His power to help those who believe in Him"* (Ephesians 1:8).

Note to Self

125

Character always trumps Genius.

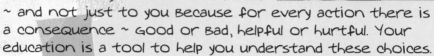

Pamela Wallin
Canadian Consul General to New York

Choice is a wonderful burden. The decisions you make will matter ~ and not just to you because for every action there is a consequence ~ good or bad, helpful or hurtful. Your education is a tool to help you understand these choices.

But your compassion is just as important. As my parents taught me, **character always trumps genius.** You can be the smartest person in the world but, it doesn't matter, if you are mean or unfair or unkind.

There are countless choices to be made in a lifetime. You can simply stand apart and watch the world go by ~ or you can choose to live and create in the world inhabited by doers and thinkers ~ people who pursue new ideas and interesting work, not just paychecks and job security.

As students, you are observers, listening and learning. But learning is not about knowing for knowing's sake. It's about knowing so we can make a difference. We want to understand why things happen and learn from that and react to it ~ that's what makes us a caring citizen ~ a participant, not just a bystander. So embrace life, take risks, find your passion and always check with both head and heart before you act.

Character
♥

Genius
✳

Character always trumps Genius.

Dr. Jerry White
President Emeritus The Navigators,
Major General USAF, Retired

Live a life of integrity and honesty.
Live a life of sexual purity.
Learn to work hard.
Always treat others with respect.
Keep from getting angry or speaking harshly
to others.
Always keep
your word and
do what you
promised
to do.

Above all,
follow God
with every-
thing you have.

Note to Self

127

Karen J. White
Insurance Broker, Kirsten's Aunt

Your life is like an open book. Each and every day of your life, pages of this book have been written and are yet to be written in the days that follow. Follow the principles that will leave each page with a message for those who read your book that is clear and inspirational. A message that leads them to live life with consistency and a zest for all that is good and right. Just think, would you want your pages to be written with laziness, selfishness, an angry spirit, dishonesty, broken relationships, disregard for truth and a life void of worship and faith?

The pages written from the day of your birth to the day of your death are but a short time in the span of history. Only you can ensure the span in-between is written with gentleness, kindness, generosity, loving relationships, worship, faithfulness and honesty which will leave a clear path to pass on these treasures of life to those who follow.

If your life's book is written this way, the life's pages of all who read your book will be influenced for good. Just think ~ you could change history!

Regent College

Dr. Rod Wilson
President, Regent College

When James talks about wisdom in James 3:13-18, he makes an interesting distinction. He suggests that there is a form of wisdom that "does not come down from heaven" (3:15) and another form of wisdom "that comes down from heaven" (3:17).

If I were going to encourage each of you in the area of wisdom, I would invite you to always think about where you get your wisdom from. In the culture, and even at times in the church, there are messages about wisdom that look right and proper. But when you examine them closely you realize that they do not find their source in God.

James makes it very clear. **The wisdom that is from heaven is "first of all pure; then peace-loving, considerate, submissive, full of mercy and good fruit, impartial and sincere."**

Make sure you find your wisdom in the right place!

Note to Self

Pastor Daniel Winter

Young Adult Ministries, Ottawa, Ontario

the MET

The story is told of two young people who, as a prank, broke into a department store one night. They didn't steal or destroy anything. They simply switched the price tags on everything. You can imagine the chaos when the store opened the next day, and the customers found diamond rings selling for $10, shaving cream for $300, an original Hummel figurine for $2, a pocket calculator for $500, umbrellas for $1000 and gold necklaces for $5.

It is so easy to get the price tags in life mixed up and to put too much importance on things and too little importance on your relationship with Jesus Christ.

If you remember one thing as you make the journey through your teenage years ~ please remember this:

Your relationship with Jesus Christ is the most important relationship in the world. It is more important than what courses you choose in high school. It is more important than the friends you have. It is even more important than the person you will marry someday. Jesus said, "But seek first the kingdom of God and His righteousness, and all these things will be added unto you." (Matthew 6:33). Remember ~ always love Jesus first and foremost. Everything else is secondary.

I have found that the greatest way to foster this relationship with Jesus is to **keep a daily spiritual journal where I record my prayers and then also I write the responses that I hear back from the Holy Spirit through God's Word ~** the Bible. If you listen to His Word and hide it in your heart, there really is a two-way conversation that takes place! That communication will build that most important relationship more than anything else.

Note to Self

Peter Wukasch
Special Education Teacher

You are important, valuaBle, and of infinite worth to your Creator and Saviour and to the people whose lives you touch. Some days we all have douBts aBout that, But when our Lord Gives us a fresh start each day, He says, *"I will never leave you nor forsake you".*

He has a destiny for you that only you are meant to fulfill. Seek to find out what that is By choosing the Lord to Be your closest friend, and listen carefully to others He sends into your life, whether your closest friends, family, employers, teachers, or youth leaders who speak Blessing and direction into your lives. They may see Gifts in you that you cannot see and skills you may not know you even have. Also try to use the words from one of God's ancient prophets, Hosea, who says, *"plant Goodness, harvest the fruit of loyalty, plow the new Ground of knowledge, and look for the Lord until He comes and pours out Goodness on you like water"* (Hosea 10:12) as your plan to start each day.

It is also important to recognize that **as Jesus took the form of a servant, we also need to have a servant's heart.** This allows Jesus to work through our personality and Gifts to draw people to Him and convince them that He is real and active.

I recall a time when I took my Behavioural Class to volunteer at the Humane Society. One of the students, who was not well-liked by the other students because he was often insensitive to their feelings, was drawn to one particular cat that was very fearful and hostile to any petting or care. He spent at least a half-hour calming this cat, talking gently to it, cuddling it, and generally caring for it. By the time we had to leave, he said that he thought he saw tears in the eyes of this cat because he had to say good-bye.

That scene forever changed my perception of this child and the Lord impressed on me for the rest of the year that He had placed this child in my teaching care so I could recognize the caring qualities he did have that I hadn't seen before, and encourage this child to show that caring to his peers.

Like I totally love cats!

Jennie

Note to Self

Try to look for the good qualities in those people you interact with and you will know the heart of God a little more.

Rev. Patricia Wynter

As we go through life, we must be very sensitive to those who travel with us on this journey. We must treat people with respect regardless of who they are. Let us always show kindness and consider what it would be like to walk in the shoes of others.

If life were all about us, how boring it would be. Who would share the laughter, the singing of the birds? Who would paint the pictures on the wall? God's guidance can be experienced everyday.

Note to Self

134

Dr. Dave B. Wyrtzen
Author and Pastor, Midlothian, Texas

Build your life on the skillful principles given to you in the Word of God. My dad and mom taught me the wisdom of God from the Old Testament Book of Proverbs from the time I was a baby. They stressed that I could only live this wisdom by inviting Jesus to come and live in my life.

I made this decision for Christ when I was five years old at Word of Life Ranch while my dad was preaching. My dad and mom didn't just "preach" about Jesus. They lived daily for Him. We knew Jesus was real because they talked to Him regularly in prayer and let Him talk to them as they read God's Word. May you have this real relationship with the biblical Jesus.

135

Dr. Philip Yancey
Author

As an exercise, I recently made a list of people who had most influenced me, whose qualities I most want to emulate. I stared at the list for some time before realizing that all have in common the surprising trait of humility.

Dr. Philip Yancey

For a time I did not appreciate humility, which I saw as an expression of negative self-image. Humble Christians seemed to grovel, parrying all compliments with "It's not me, it's the Lord." And as a nerdy mathematician friend of mine once expressed it, the humble are a self-wallowing set: when you become conscious of belonging, you're immediately excluded.

Yet I now see that neither complaint applies to the people I most admire. A great scientist, a splendid poet, a theologian who works with the poor ~ none has a negative self-image. All excelled in school, won awards, and have little reason to doubt their gifts and abilities. Humility is, for them, an ongoing choice to credit God, not themselves, for their natural gifts and then to use those gifts in God's service.

Humility has many dimensions. My first employer showed it in the kind and patient way he treated me, a writer still wet behind the ears. He never made an editorial change without painstakingly convincing me that the change would actually improve my piece.

He saw his mission as not just to improve articles but to improve writers.

Other heroes of mine exercise humility by finding a group overlooked and underserved. I think of Dr. Paul Brand, a promising young physician who volunteered in India as the first orthopedic surgeon to work with leprosy patients. Or of Henri Nouwen, professor at Notre Dame, Yale and Harvard, who ended up among people having a fraction of those students' IQs; the mentally handicapped at L'Arche homes in France and Toronto. Both of these men demonstrated to me that **downward mobility can lead to the success that matters most.**

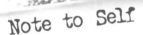

Note to Self

Kirsten with Dr. and Mrs. Zacharias.

Margaret Zacharias

Vice-President, Ravi Zacharias
International Ministries

Ask God to keep your
heart open toward Him,
soft and moldable, so
that He never has to
break you to accomplish
His will in your life.

Note to Self

138

Dr. Ravi Zacharias

Founder, Ravi Zacharias International Ministries, Author

FORGET... REMEMBER... STAND

You must learn to <u>forget</u> the petty hurts and disappointments that come your way. Often we are hurt by friends or by someone's unkind words or actions. Close the door on those memories so that they don't make you bitter or negative.

Always <u>remember</u> who you are ~ a child of God. You are uniquely made by Him. There is no one else like you. God fashioned you as a person with distinct skills and a personality all your own. Remember you are His child and your example must reflect His love in your life.

Do not give in to the pressures of culture and other influences that take you away from God's Word. <u>Stand</u> on the convictions that He has given to us in the Scriptures. That is the foundation on which your life must be built.

You are young now, but the years will go by quickly. What you forget, **what you remember and now, how you stand will lead you into the future.** May God bless you so that you will do what is right.

139.

Tim Zimmerman

Director, The King's Brass

Remember that there is a God who is smiling on you because of His grace. You can laugh and swim in the happiness of this loving God.

Don't ever loose sight of your dreams. Closed doors are only to test your resolve. Work hard to be able to do what you love for the rest of your life.

Finally, the real world is the one that can't be touched with our five senses. It is an immense kingdom controlled by the hand of God. Live in this kingdom world, learn to love well, and your feet will be on solid ground.

Note to Self